THE
WALKING DEAD
ULTIMATE QUIZ BOOK

Jack Goldstein
&
Frankie Taylor

ACORN BOOKS

Unofcial and Unauthorised

Published in 2016 by
Acorn Books
www.acornbooks.co.uk

Acorn Books is an imprint of
Andrews UK Limited
www.andrewsuk.com

Contents

Contents - Continued

Introduction

We won't keep you long, as you're bound to want to dive straight into the quiz. So all we'd like to do in this brief introduction is to let you know that the vast majority of questions relate purely to the *TV series*. As the differences between this and the comic are so vast, we make a point of mentioning the comic books when the question relates to them. Hopefully that clarifies things for you... and all but the most pedantic fan should be able to figure this out as they go anyway. Good luck and have fun!

The Quiz

Questions

Pot Luck - Part 1

Some general questions to warm you up...

1. What is Ty's signature weapon?

2. Who is the only person to have killed more people than Rick?

3. Name Gareth's mother.

4. What was the name of Sasha's 'survivalist nut' neighbour?

5. Name Morgan's wife.

6. Which game is Deanna particularly skilled at?

7. Who, other than Glenn, caught the illness in the prison but was still alive at the end of season six?

8. True or false: Tara is the second character in the TV series to have been introduced in a flashback?

9. What did Andrea study at university?

10. True or false: Gabriel believed that Rick's group was sent by God to punish him?

Name the Season - Part 1

In which season were the following episodes broadcast?

11. *Vatos*

12. *I Ain't a Judas*

13. *Self Help*

14. *Internment*

15. *When the Dead Come Knocking*

16. *Save the Last One*

17. *Try*

18. *Home*

19. *Us*

20. *The Distance*

Which Character - Part 1

Which character is played by the following actors & actresses?

21. James Allen McCune

22. Michael Rooker

23. Benedict Samuel

24. Jordan Woods-Robinson

25. Melissa Ponzio

26. Danai Gurira

27. Alanna Masterson

28. Dallas Roberts

29. Daniel Thomas May

30. Major Dodson

Character Round - Rick

Time to focus on one main character now. For this round, it's Rick...

31. With which Sheriff's department was Rick a police officer?

32. True or false: Rick sees himself as a committed Catholic?

33. Who does Rick become romantically involved with after executing her husband?

34. In which war did Rick's grandfather fight?

35. What object does Rick keep as a memento of his father?

36. Where on Rick's body is he shot, leading to his coma?

37. What is Rick's signature weapon?

38. Is Rick left or right-handed?

39. True or false: Rick is the first character in the TV show to directly kill a living person?

40. What is Rick's blood type?

Season's Meetings - Part 1

In which season are we first introduced to the following characters?

41.   Andrea

42.   Dale Horvath

43.   Fr. Gabriel Stokes

44.   Lori Grimes

45.   Gareth

46.   Michonne

47.   Hershel Greene

48.   Beth Greene

49.   Jessie Anderson

50.   Shane Walsh

Pot Luck - Part 2

More general knowledge here...

51. Why did Dale and his wife never have a child?

52. From which country do Hershel's family originate?

53. With what animal did Abraham have a 'messy experience' which resulted in it exploding?

54. Who previously owned the house in which Morgan and his family initially took refuge post-apocalypse?

55. What is Tara's weapon of choice?

56. Who is the first living character we see in the whole show?

57. True or false: Eugene and Abraham *do* eventually apologise to each other?

58. What job was Tara training for before the apocalypse happened?

59. Who was the last surviving member of Martinez's camp?

60. In which episode are we first introduced to Rosita?

So Many Ways to Die

Whose deaths are we describing here?

61.　Tragically shot by Dawn after stabbing her with scissors...

62.　Killed by her sister in an attempt to prove that the living and the dead are no different...

63.　Stabbed by his partner and one-time best friend after luring him into the middle of the forest under the pretext of a search...

64.　Savaged by a walker that forced itself into his tent...

65.　Handed a gun so she could take her own life after being captured and bitten on the neck...

66.　Left to turn after being stabbed in the stomach four times by The Governor for his betrayal...

67.　Shot in the leg by Carol as she opens the door, leaving the walkers to finish the job...

68.　Stomach slit by a wolf after being told to smoke a cigarette outside...

69.　Has throat slit 'accidentally' by an agitated and intoxicated Pete after trying to calm him down...

70.　After Nicholas panics in a revolving door, this character is dragged out by their leg...

Anagrams - Part 1

The names of some well-known characters from the series are jumbled up below... but can you unscramble them?

71.   Sicker Grim

72.   Daemon Noire

73.   Shawn Heals

74.   Green Thebe

75.   Sob Took Bye

76.   La Swish Salami

77.   Menagerie Egg

78.   Nonces Emperor

79.   Hairiest People

80.   Mo Grislier

Who Plays - Part 1

Can you name the actor or actress who plays each of the following roles?

81. Dr. Denise Cloyd

82. Mary

83. Amy

84. Hershel Greene

85. Phillip Blake

86. Noah

87. Lt. Dawn Lerner

88. Nicholas

89. Aiden Monroe

90. Ron Anderson

Quotes - Part 1

Who said the following lines?

91. "Some people just can't give up. Like us."

92. "That's the third time you're pointing that thing at my head. You gonna pull the trigger or what?!"

93. "I hear Nebraska is nice."

94. "Four men, four rounds. What are the odds, huh? Let's just hope four is your lucky number."

95. "Jesus promised a resurrection of the dead. I just thought he had something a little different in mind."

96. "Rick and his group, they're not good people. They've done things. They've done unspeakable things."

97. "I may have lost my hand, but you lost your sense of direction."

98. "The world ended. Didn't you get the memo?"

99. "Nightmares end. They shouldn't end who you are. And that is just this dead man's opinion."

100. "People like you are supposed to be dead, except that these walls went up just in time."

Character Round - Daryl

Time now for a round wholly dedicated to Daryl...

101. Who is Daryl's brother?

102. Which item of Beth's does Daryl keep as a memento?

103. What nickname does Carol give Daryl in the season four premier?

104. In which episode are we first introduced to Daryl?

105. During a game of *Never Have I Ever* (as Beth refers to it), Daryl confesses he has never set foot out of which state?

106. What is Daryl's signature weapon?

107. In the episode *Home* we see multiple scars across Daryl's back; what are they the result of?

108. What did Beth assume Daryl's job was pre-apocalypse?

109. How many days did Daryl spend lost in the woods as a child?

110. And during this period, what did he use as a substitute for toilet paper?

Pot Luck - Part 3

Where this round goes, nobody knows...

111. With how many other scientists did Eugene claim he was working with in his work combatting diseases?

112. Is Abraham left- or right-handed?

113. True or false: Bob Stookey suffers from alcoholism?

114. Which body parts is Merle missing?

115. What foodstuff did Lori make on Sundays, despite knowing that they were awful?

116. Name Shane's grandmother.

117. True or false: The Governor was an only child?

118. What was Deanna's job pre-apocalypse?

119. Which number did Shane play in his school's football team?

120. Name Andrea's sister.

Which Character - Part 2

Another chance to answer who in the show is portrayed by the following fantastic actors & actresses...

121. Christian Serratos

122. Lennie James

123. Sonequa Martin-Green

124. Audrey Marie Anderson

125. Josh McDermitt

126. Lew Temple

127. Seth Gilliam

128. Alexandra Breckenridge

129. Jeryl Prescott Sales

130. Lawrence Gilliard, Jr.

Character Round - Maggie

Let's dedicate this round to the one and only Maggie...

131. What does Maggie call the walkers in the barn?

132. Whose baby does Maggie deliver?

133. True or false: Maggie's family initially believed that walkers were just simply sick people.

134. True or False: Maggie's mother was bitten by a walker?

135. Apart from Merle, and one of the Cannibals from the terminus, who else has kidnapped Maggie?

136. How does The Governor get Maggie to reveal the location of the camp?

137. Who does Maggie bar from the house over Beth's suicide attempt?

138. Where is Maggie when she reveals her pregnancy to Aaron?

139. When the farmhouse is running low on supplies, who does Rick suggest Maggie take with her on a supply run into town?

140. When Gabriel is shocked at the group's violence, saying the church is 'God's House', what is Maggie's reply?

Season's Meetings - Part 2

Again, in which season did we first meet...

141. Dr. Eugene Porter

142. Sasha Williams

143. Bob Stookey

144. Spencer Monroe

145. Rick Grimes

146. Deanna Monroe

147. Sgt. Abraham Ford

148. Maggie Greene

149. Tyreese Williams

150. Morgan Jones

Name the Season - Part 2

And another season-focused round; which season featured these gripping episodes?

151. *Seed*

152. *Triggerfinger*

153. *Crossed*

154. *Inmates*

155. *Days Gone Bye*

156. *Nebraska*

157. *Bloodletting*

158. *Guts*

159. *Dead Weight*

160. *Tell It to the Frogs*

Pot Luck - Part 4

You'll either love them or hate them, but there's no getting away from these pot luck rounds...

161. In which city did Sasha live before the apocalypse?

162. Name Aaron's partner, who he met through his work.

163. At which church was Gabriel a priest?

164. What caused Abraham's violent retaliation against his initial post-apocalyptic colleagues?

165. What is The Governor's weapon of choice?

166. True or false: Jessie has no tattoos?

167. What does Lori have tattooed on her abdomen?

168. What was Gabriel's 'dark secret'?

169. The patches on Bob Stookey's jacket represent which two divisions?

170. What is Aaron's signature weapon?

Character Round - Carol

How much do you know about this initially introverted character?

171. With whom did Carol evacuate to Atlanta during the initial outbreak?

172. True or False: Carol is a devout Christian?

173. Why is Carol exiled by Rick?

174. And what does she do that regains his respect?

175. Who does Carol threaten for getting in her way of killing the leader of the Wolves?

176. True or False: Carol is the longest-living female character, as of Season six?

177. Which phobia does Carol suffer from, albeit to a minor extent?

178. What is considered to be Carol's Weapon of choice?

179. Name the episode in which Carol first appeared.

180. What type of flower does Daryl give to Carol after searching for Sophia?

Who Plays - Part 2

The second round in the 'Who Plays' series... just name the actor or actress that gets themselves into character as...

181. Patrick

182. Paul "Jesus" Rovia

183. Shumpert

184. Sophia Peletier

185. Martin

186. Daryl Dixon

187. Aaron

188. Morales

189. Caleb Subramanian

190. Abraham Ford

Anagrams - Part 2

More mixed-up characters here; can you rearrange these letters correctly?

191. SEO Aspirations

192. Altar Chamber

193. Red Session Jean

194. Exiled Norm

195. Reanimates Czar

196. Fo Drama Brah

197. Sheer Glen Here

198. Kill Blip Heap

199. Anon Enamored

200. I, Odd Larynx

Quotes - Part 2

Another chance to demonstrate your perfect recollection of the show's script! Who said...

201. "I'll bake 'em a cake. with pink frosting."

202. "You walk outside, you risk your life. You take a drink of water, you risk your life. Nowadays you breath and you risk your life. You don't have a choice. The only thing you can choose is what you're risking it for."

203. "The world we know is gone, but keeping our humanity? That's a choice."

204. "People in hell want Slurpees."

205. "Running is not an option."

206. "If I had known the world was ending, I'd have brought better books."

207. "It's the same as it ever was: the weak get taken."

208. "Nice moves there, Clint Eastwood. You're the new sheriff come riding in to clean up the town?"

209. "I see a chance to make a new start."

210. "Just because we're good people does not mean we won't kill you."

NaMe the Killer

Who killed the following characters?

211. Dale Horvath

212. Hershel Greene

213. Owen (The Wolves)

214. Merle Dixon

215. Pete Anderson

216. Nicholas

217. Theodore Douglas (T-Dog)

218. Lizzie Samuels

219. Betsy

220. Gareth

Pot Luck - Part 5

You should know the drill by now...

221. Which weapon does Gabriel choose?

222. While brushing his daughter's hair and on two other occasions, The Governor is seen listening to classical music. Who is the music's composer?

223. True or false: Rosita had a nine-year old nephew?

224. Jessie attended a particular type of educational establishment when she was younger. Was it a) stage school, or b) art school?

225. How does Hershel survive the infection, becoming the first person to do so?

226. Who is the last person to die in season five?

227. Which illegal drug does Merle tell Daryl he is looking for?

228. True or False: Hershel never directly killed another living human?

229. What killed Merle's mother?

230. Name Tara's older sister.

Which Character - Part 3

Some tricky ones in here; who is portrayed by the following actors & actresses?

231. Melissa McBride

232. Chad L. Coleman

233. Andrew Rothenberg

234. Jason Douglas

235. Jon Bernthal

236. Sarah Wayne Callies

237. Andrew Lincoln

238. Andrew J. West

239. Lauren Cohan

240. Kyla Kenedy

Name the Season - Part 3

True fans know each episode by name... so which series featured the following?

241. *Prey*

242. *After*

243. *18 Miles Out*

244. *Clear*

245. *TS-19*

246. *Coda*

247. *What Lies Ahead*

248. *Killer Within*

249. *The Suicide King*

250. *Strangers*

Character Round - Beth

It's Beth time!

251. True or False: Beth's counterpart in the comic series is half her TV character's age?

252. What instrument did Beth used to play well when she was a young child?

253. What is engraved on the silver spoon that Beth finds?

254. Who sees Beth playing the guitar in their hallucination?

255. Who forces Beth to eat a lollipop?

256. Name one of the two characters with whom Beth has a semi-romantic relationship.

257. How old is Beth when we first meet her in the TV series?

258. What is the name of the last episode in which Beth appears?

259. Can you name Beth's cousin?

260. True or False: Beth moved to the farm when she was just three years old?

Pot Luck - Part 6

How much attention do you pay to every single line spoken, and everything you see on screen? Let's find out...

261. In which city did Aaron live pre-apocalypse?

262. Where did Abraham first make a base from which to survive the outbreak?

263. What's Rosita's surname?

264. What was Sasha's job pre-apocalypse?

265. Who said this, and to whom: "You think you're the law?! You actually think you have a say in anything here?!"

266. When Glenn fixes the broken-down RV, what is wrong with it?

267. True or false: Abraham was a military colonel?

268. What is Abraham's signature weapon?

269. Who does Merle call 'Taco Bender'?

270. What did Shane steal that belonged to his principal as a prank when he was at school?

Quotes - Part 3

It's quote time again! Who said the following...

271. "But sooner or later, you get cornered. You wind up stayin' and you wind up killin'. We don't go back. We can't go back."

272. "The pain doesn't go away. You just make room for it."

273. "Waste of an arrow."

274. "I didn't turn away. I kept listening to the news so I could do what I could to help. I'm not giving up."

275. "Today, we're talking about knives. How to use them, how to be safe with them, how they could save your life."

276. "You can't think forever. Sooner or later, you gotta make a move."

277. "You can't just be the good guy and expect to live. Not anymore."

278. "There are some things you don't come back from. You either live with them, or you don't."

279. "You knew how to bite a dick!"

280. "If I had known the world was ending, I would have brought better books."

Who Plays - Part 3

What is the name of the person who plays the following characters in The Walking Dead?

281. Enid

282. Reg Monroe

283. Joe

284. Gregory

285. Dr. Steven Edwards

286. Andrea

287. Ben

288. Glenn Rhee

289. Otis

290. Ed Peletier

Character Round - Glenn

It wouldn't be the ultimate *quiz if there wasn't a round about Glenn...*

291. Who does Glenn marry?

292. What is Glenn's role at the Alexandria Safe-Zone?

293. According to Glenn, who saved him before he joined up with the rest of the Atlanta Camp survivors?

294. Glenn's family hail from Michigan, but from which country do they actually *originate* from?

295. True or false: The surname *Rhee* is never mentioned in the TV Series?

296. Who else has been captured three times (up to the end of season six), the same number as Glenn?

297. What was Glenn's job pre-apocalypse?

298. True or false: Glenn only ever had brothers?

299. What does Hershel say to Glenn when giving him his grandfather's watch?

300. Who does Glenn suggest using as a bargaining chip for The Governor?

Anagrams - Part 3

One last chance to unscramble the anagrams to find the names of characters featured in the show...

301. Use Sizzle Mail

302. Eerily Slim Waste

303. Do Doghouse Later

304. Jargon Omens

305. Hardhat Love

306. Earpiece Troll

307. Blokes Gaiters

308. Rogue Preteen

309. Momma Litten

310. Girl Scream

Pot Luck - Part 7

More random questions about more random things...

311. True or false: Shane was the first character in the TV series to cause the death of another living character?

312. Name Tara's father.

313. For how many years had Hershel's farm been in his family's hands: 100, 160, 190 or 210?

314. What is Morgan's signature weapon?

315. How and when did The Governor's wife die?

316. Name The Governor's daughter.

317. What is The Governor's real name?

318. What is the name of the horse ridden by Daryl that throws him off when spooked by a snake?

319. Which band's logo is displayed on Sasha's shirt when we first meet her?

320. Who previously owned Daryl's motorcycle?

Season's Meetings - Part 3

Which season brought these characters into our lives?

321. Rosita Espinosa

322. Aaron

323. Carl Grimes

324. Carol Peletier

325. The Governor/Phillip Blake

326. Glenn Rhee

327. Tara Chambler

328. Daryl Dixon

329. Merle Dixon

330. T-Dog

Character Round - Michonne

How much do you know about Michonne?

331. What was the name of Michonne's son?

332. And how old was he when he died?

333. What is her signature weapon?

334. When we are first introduced to Michonne she has two pet walkers on chains; both their arms are amputated. Who are they?

335. In that episode, she is hidden by a hood and cape. The reason for this was that the actress hadn't yet been cast. True or False?

336. And what was the name of that episode?

337. Which member of the group does Michonne first become friends with?

338. Michonne and Andrea investigate a plume of smoke. What did it turn out to be?

339. What is the name of the horse that Michonne is seen riding back from a scouting trip?

340. What does Michonne give to Carl on the proviso that he gives the back to her when he's finished with them?

Quotes - Part 4

One last time: who said the following?

341. "You fight it. You don't give up. And one day you just change."

342. "I didn't ask for this. I killed my best friend for you people."

343. "Anger makes you stupid. Stupid gets you killed."

344. "I know how the safety works."

345. "We didn't come here for the eggs."

346. "Do what you're gonna do. Then go to hell."

347. "You grow up country you pick up a thing or two."

348. "Good thing we didn't do anything stupid like shoot it."

349. "We don't kill the living."

350. "Why are we running? What are we doing?"

Name the Season - Part 4

One final time: in which season were these episodes broadcast?

351. *Claimed*

352. *Chupacabra*

353. *Walk with Me*

354. *Wildfire*

355. *Hounded*

356. *Alone*

357. *A*

358. *Secrets*

359. *What Happened and What's Going On*

360. *Beside the Dying Fire*

Which Character - Part 4

These are the names of actors and actresses who play characters in the TV series. But which ones?

361. Jeffrey DeMunn

362. Meyrick Murphy

363. Chandler Riggs

364. Michael Zegen

365. Emily Kinney

366. Jose Pablo Cantillo

367. Tovah Feldshuh

368. Corey Hawkins

369. Austin Nichols

370. Corey Brill

Who Am I?

Each question below is a brief description of a particular character... but which one?

371. I lost my wife and son. Grief-stricken, I then killed anyone and everyone who crossed my path, dead or alive. It's thanks to Eastman that I am now a changed man...

372. The last thing I remember is being told to look at the flowers...

373. I said "I mean, I get that you'll just have to take my word for this but, she wasn't even the one I was aiming for"...

374. I am the last surviving member of the Greene family...

375. Before the apocalypse began, I was a wife and mother to four daughters. My time at work was spent reading inspirational emails to get me through the day...

376. I said "You don't know what it's like out there. You may think you do but you don't!"...

377. I have excellent knowledge of the department store sewage system due to my previous job with the city's zoning office...

378. Born into the apocalyptic world, my name was *nearly* Sophia...

379. After turning, I was kept locked up in my dad's apartment. He wanted to believe I was still alive...

380. I said "When I sent my people to kill your people for killing my people... you killed more of my people. Not cool"...

About the Show

Testing your knowledge of the show itself here...

381. Name the three people behind the comic book on which the TV series is based.

382. On what date did the show premiere in the US?

383. What is the name of the companion show first broadcast on AMC in August 2015 that follows a different set of characters?

384. Who is mainly responsible for the music you hear?

385. In which state is the show mostly filmed?

386. When the show debuted, how many major cities were involved in the 'worldwide zombie invasion' marketing event?

387. True or False: *The Walking Dead* won a Golden Globe award in 2010 for 'Best Television Series (Drama)'?

388. Which network famously passed on the show, believing it was too violent?

389. True or False: Neither Daryl nor Merle nor Sasha have counterpart characters in the comic book series?

390. Which roll did Norman Reedus initially audition for?

Character Round - Carl

It's the last character-specific round of the quiz. It's Carl...

391. True or False: Initially Carl believed his father to be dead?

392. Of what type of weapon does Carl find an arsenal in the second season?

393. Who accidentally shoots Carl?

394. Which former friend does Carl say he would have put down himself?

395. On whom does Carl develop a crush during season three?

396. Who does Carl chastise for believing the walkers are not so different to the living?

397. What is Carl's blood type?

398. What did Carl drink in third grade that nearly made him throw up?

399. True or False: Carl was in favour of letting Gabriel die?

400. What did Carl give to Maggie to help her grieve over Beth's death?

Pot Luck - Part 8

We're nearly there...

401. True or false: Ty shoots and wields his chosen weapon with his left hand?

402. Who does Eugene first tell that he sabotaged the bus?

403. Why did Sasha and her brother leave their neighbour's bunker?

404. What role did Bob Stookey have in the army, pre-apocalypse?

405. Who hits Rick in the face with a shovel, mistaking him for a zombie?

406. Which friend did Paula confide in when she was facing marital difficulties?

407. What is Shane's signature weapon?

408. Who is appointed alongside Rick as a constable by Deanna Monroe?

409. How many years are there between Andrea and her sister?

410. True or False: Ty was a former NBA player?

The Final Few

We hope you're enjoyed the quiz! Here's your last ten questions...

411. Who initially rescued Andrea when we first meet her?

412. Why was Merle dishonourably discharged from the army?

413. In which state did Spencer live pre-apocalypse?

414. Where on his body does Morgan have a tattoo of his wife?

415. Who is Ty's younger sister?

416. With whom did Ty have a relationship in the prison?

417. What was Dale's wife's name?

418. Which of The Governor's eyes is injured?

419. With whom did Lori have an affair?

420. Name Hershel's first wife.

Answers

Pot Luck - Part 1

1. A hammer

2. The Governor

3. Mary

4. Jerry

5. Jenny

6. Poker

7. Sasha

8. False. She is actually the first.

9. Law

10. True

Name the Season - Part 1

11.   First

12.   Third

13.   Fifth

14.   Fourth

15.   Third

16.   Second

17.   Fifth

18.   Third

19.   Fourth

20.   Fifth

Which Character - Part 1

21. Jimmy

22. Merle Dixon

23. Wolf

24. Eric Raleigh

25. Karen

26. Michonne

27. Tara Chambler

28. Milton Mamet

29. Allen

30. Sam Anderson

Character Round - Rick

31.   King County Sheriff's Department

32.   False. He sees religion as a waste of time.

33.   Jessie Anderson

34.   The Second World War

35.   A watch

36.   His shoulder

37.   A Colt Python .357 Magnum caliber revolver

38.   He is actually ambidextrous, although generally seems to favour his right hand.

39.   True. Although Shane caused the death of Otis, he wasn't directly responsible.

40.   A+

Season's Meetings - Part 1

41. 1

42. 1

43. 5

44. 1

45. 4

46. 2

47. 2

48. 2

49. 5

50. 1

Pot Luck - Part 2

51.   The first time they tried, she miscarried; she later
        succumbed to cancer.

52.   Ireland

53.   A camel

54.   Fred and Cindy Drakes

55.   A Smith & Wesson M&P

56.   Rick

57.   True

58.   Police officer

59.   Tara

60.   *Inmates*

So Many Ways to Die

61. Beth Greene

62. Mika Samuels

63. Shane Walsh

64. Ed Peletier

65. Andrea

66. Milton Mamet

67. Mary

68. Shelly Neudermeyer

69. Reg Monroe

70. Noah

Anagrams - Part 1

71. Rick Grimes

72. Aiden Monroe

73. Shane Walsh

74. Beth Greene

75. Bob Stookey

76. Sasha Williams

77. Maggie Greene

78. Spencer Monroe

79. Sophia Peletier

80. Lori Grimes

Who Plays - Part 1

81.   Merritt Wever

82.   Denise Crosby

83.   Emma Bell

84.   Scott Wilson

85.   David Morrissey

86.   Tyler James Williams

87.   Christine Woods

88.   Michael Traynor

89.   Daniel Bonjour

90.   Austin Abrams

Quotes - Part 1

91. Carol

92. Daryl

93. Rick

94. Shane

95. Hershel

96. Gabriel

97. Merle

98. Amy

99. Bob

100. Glenn

Character Round - Daryl

101. Merle

102. Her hunting knife

103. Pookie

104. *Tell it to the Frogs*

105. Georgia

106. A crossbow

107. His abusive father

108. Motorcycle mechanic

109. Nine

110. Poison oak

Pot Luck - Part 3

111. Nine

112. Left-handed

113. True

114. His right hand and two fingers from his left hand.

115. Pancakes

116. Jean

117. False – he had a brother

118. A congresswomen in Ohio

119. 22

120. Amy

Which Character - Part 2

121. Rosita Espinosa

122. Morgan Jones

123. Sasha Williams

124. Lilly Chambler

125. Dr. Eugene Porter

126. Axel

127. Fr. Gabriel Stokes

128. Jessie Anderson

129. Jacqui

130. Bob Stookey

Character Round - Maggie

131. Mom, Shawn, Mr and Mrs Fisher, Laci, and Duncan

132. Lori's

133. True

134. False. She died when Maggie was young.

135. The Saviours (specifically Paula)

136. He threatens to shoot Glenn.

137. Andrea

138. A sewer

139. Glenn

140. That it is simply four walls and a roof.

Season's Meetings - Part 2

141. 4

142. 3

143. 4

144. 5

145. 1

146. 5

147. 4

148. 2

149. 3

150. 1

Name the Season - Part 2

151. Third

152. Second

153. Fifth

154. Fourth

155. First

156. Second

157. Second

158. First

159. Fourth

160. First

Pot Luck - Part 4

161. Jacksonville, Florida

162. Eric Raleigh

163. St. Sarah's Episcopal Church

164. Their rape of his wife

165. A Beretta 92SB Nickel – although he does also sometimes use a Steyr AUG A1.

166. False. In fact she has at least two.

167. A butterfly

168. Not letting other survivors in the church in the days following the outbreak.

169. The 82nd Airborne and 1st Armored Divisions

170. A machete

Character Round - Carol

171. Her husband Ed and daughter Sophia

172. True... until season five. She is often seen praying for her and her daughter's safety, but later reveals that she is no longer sure about her beliefs.

173. For killing two sick members of the group, something Rick deemed morally questionable.

174. She wipes out the Terminus compound.

175. Morgan

176. True

177. Claustrophobia

178. Her trench knife

179. *Tell it to the Frogs*

180. A Cherokee Rose

Who Plays - Part 2

181. Vincent Martella

182. Tom Payne

183. Travis Love

184. Madison Lintz

185. Chris Coy

186. Norman Reedus

187. Ross Marquand

188. Juan Pareja

189. Sunkrish Bala

190. Michael Cudlitz

Anagrams - Part 2

191. Rosita Espinosa

192. Tara Chambler

193. Jessie Anderson

194. Merle Dixon

195. Caesar Martinez

196. Abraham Ford

197. Hershel Greene

198. Phillip Blake

199. Deanna Monroe

200. Daryl Dixon

Quotes - Part 2

201. Merle

202. Hershel

203. Dale

204. Daryl

205. Glenn

206. Dale

207. Guillermo

208. Glenn

209. Dale

210. Rick

Name the Killer

211. A Walker (wound)

212. The Governor

213. Morgan

214. The Governor

215. Rick

216. Himself (suicide)

217. A Walker (bitten)

218. Carol Peletier

219. Herself (suicide)

220. Rick

Pot Luck - Part 5

221. A machete

222. Chopin

223. False. He was six.

224. b) Art school

225. He has his leg amputated?

226. Pete Anderson

227. Crystal Meth

228. True

229. A house fire, itself caused by a cigarette she fell asleep smoking

230. Lilly

Which Character - Part 3

231. Carol Peletier

232. Tyreese Williams

233. Jim

234. Tobin

235. Shane Walsh

236. Lori Grimes

237. Rick Grimes

238. Gareth

239. Maggie Greene

240. Mika Samuels

Name the Season - Part 3

241. Third

242. Fourth

243. Second

244. Third

245. First

246. Fifth

247. Second

248. Third

249. Third

250. Fifth

Character Round - Beth

251. False. In fact, she has no comic counterpart!

252. The piano

253. Washington D.C.

254. Tyreese

255. Gorman

256. Jimmy or Zach.

257. Sixteen

258. *Forget* (although she was killed in *Coda*, she appears in this later episode as a hallucination)

259. Arnold Greene

260. False. She's lived there all her life.

Pot Luck - Part 6

261. Washington D.C.

262. A grocery store

263. Espinosa

264. Firefighter

265. Pete to Rick

266. A dead battery

267. False. He was only a sergeant.

268. An M-16 assault rifle

269. Morales

270. His car

Quotes - Part 3

Who Plays - Part 3

281. Katelyn Nacon

282. Steve Coulter

283. Jeff Kober

284. Xander Berkeley

285. Erik Jensen

286. Laurie Holden

287. Tyler Chase

288. Steven Yeun

289. Pruitt Taylor Vince

290. Adam Minarovich

Character Round - Glenn

291. Maggie

292. A supply runner

293. T-Dog

294. Korea

295. True. However, it is listed as such on the official website.

296. Maggie

297. He delivered pizzas.

298. False. He has spoken about his mother and sisters, although their fate is currently unknown

299. "No man is good enough for your little girl until one is."

300. Merle

Anagrams - Part 3

301. Lizzie Samuels

302. Tyreese Williams

303. Theodore Douglas

304. Morgan Jones

305. Dale Horvath

306. Carol Peletier

307. Gabriel Stokes

308. Eugene Porter

309. Milton Mamet

310. Carl Grimes

Pot Luck - Part 7

311. True. It was Otis.

312. David

313. 160

314. A wooden staff (crafted by Eastman)

315. In a car accident, a year and a half prior to the apocalypse.

316. Penny

317. Philip Blake

318. Nervous Nellie

319. Southern Gothic Revival

320. Merle

Season's Meetings - Part 3

Character Round - Michonne

331. Andre

332. Three

333. A katana

334. Her boyfriend and his friend (Mike and Terry)

335. True

336. *Beside The Dying Fire*

337. Andrea

338. A helicopter

339. Flame

340. Comic books

Quotes - Part 4

341. Carol

342. Rick

343. Michonne

344. Andrea

345. Andrew

346. Maggie

347. Maggie

348. T-Dog

349. Rick

350. Carl

Name the Season - Part 4

351. Fourth

352. Second

353. Third

354. First

355. Third

356. Fourth

357. Fourth

358. Second

359. Fifth

360. Second

Which Character - Part 4

361. Dale Horvath

362. Meghan Chambler

363. Carl Grimes

364. Randall

365. Beth Greene

366. Caesar Martinez

367. Deanna Monroe

368. Heath

369. Spencer Monroe

370. Pete Anderson

Who Am I?

371. Morgan

372. Lizzie Samuels

373. Dwight

374. Maggie Greene

375. Paula

376. Rick

377. Jacqui

378. Judith Grimes

379. Penny

380. Negan

About the Show

381. Robert Kirkman, Tony Moore and Charlie Adlard.

382. The 31st of October, 2010

383. *Fear the Walking Dead*

384. Bear McCreary

385. Georgia

386. 26

387. False. The show was nominated in that category though.

388. HBO

389. True

390. Merle

Character Round - Carl

391. True

392. Knives

393. Otis

394. Sophia

395. Beth

396. Lizzie

397. A+, the same as his father's.

398. Soya milk

399. False. It is actually Carl who insists they help him.

400. A music box

PotLuck - Part 8

401. False. Although he shoots with his left hand, he uses his right hand for the hammer.

402. Tara

403. They had run out of supplies.

404. Medic

405. Duane Jones

406. Paula

407. A Glock 17, although he does also regularly use a Mossberg 590.

408. Michonne.

409. Twelve

410. False. He was actually a sportsman in the NFL.

The Final Few

411. Dale

412. He punched a sergeant

413. Ohio

414. On his right shoulder

415. Sasha

416. Karen

417. Irma

418. His right eye.

419. Shane

420. Josephine

You may also enjoy...

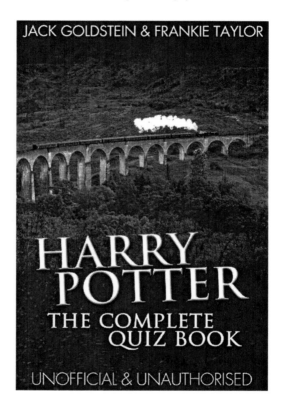

JACK GOLDSTEIN & FRANKIE TAYLOR

HARRY POTTER
THE COMPLETE
QUIZ BOOK

UNOFFICIAL & UNAUTHORISED

Lightning Source UK Ltd.
Milton Keynes UK
UKOW02f1815161216
290160UK00001B/33/P